# The Glucose Revolution Cookbook for Beginners

## The Perfect Combination of Recipes, Tips and Strategies for Balancing and Maintaining Blood Sugar Levels

LUCY EVANS

# Contents

**5 Chapter 5: Smart Snacks and Desserts: Indulge Without Compromising Your Blood Sugar**     **65**

**6 What's Next? Grab Your Free Bonuses!**     **75**

# Welcome to The Glucose Revolution!

In an age where dietary choices and health are more interconnected than ever, managing blood sugar levels has emerged as a crucial aspect of overall well-being. The rise in chronic conditions such as diabetes and metabolic syndrome highlights the importance of understanding and controlling our blood sugar levels, not just as a necessity but as a means to enhance our quality of life. Welcome to *The Glucose Revolution Cookbook for Beginners*, a comprehensive guide designed to empower you on your journey towards balanced blood sugar and vibrant health.

This book is not just a collection of recipes; it is a celebration of a lifestyle that harmoniously integrates delicious food with mindful health practices. Here, we aim to transform the way you think about managing your blood sugar by demonstrating that it is entirely possible to enjoy a diverse array of meals while keeping your glucose levels in check. With a focus on simplicity, flavor, and nutrition, each recipe in this cookbook has been meticulously crafted to support your journey towards optimal blood sugar balance.

## Understanding Blood Sugar Balance

To embark on this journey, it's essential to grasp the fundamentals of blood sugar balance. Blood sugar, or glucose, is the primary source of energy for our bodies. However, fluctuations in blood sugar levels can impact our overall health, energy, and mood. This book starts with a comprehensive exploration of how blood sugar works, the role of insulin, and the factors influencing blood sugar levels. Understanding these principles will empower you to make informed decisions about your diet and lifestyle.

## Eating Well: A Delicious Approach to Blood Sugar Management

One of the core philosophies of this cookbook is that managing blood sugar does not mean sacrificing flavor or enjoyment. The recipes presented here are designed to showcase the vibrant possibilities within a blood sugar-friendly diet. From colorful salads to hearty mains and indulgent desserts, each dish is crafted to provide balanced nutrition while delighting your palate. We believe that healthy eating should be a pleasure, not a chore, and we're committed to proving that you can savor every bite while keeping your blood sugar levels stable.

## Crafting a Lifestyle: Beyond the Plate

Achieving optimal blood sugar balance extends beyond the kitchen. It involves incorporating lifestyle habits that support overall health and well-being. This book provides guidance on integrating regular physical activity, effective stress management, and adequate sleep into your daily routine. Each section is designed to offer practical tips and strategies that complement your dietary choices, creating a holistic approach to health.

## A Journey of Discovery

*The Glucose Revolution Cookbook for Beginners* is more than just a guide—it is an invitation to embark on a journey of discovery and empowerment. Whether you are newly diagnosed with blood sugar concerns or seeking to refine your current approach to health, this book offers a wealth of information and inspiration. You'll find yourself exploring new ingredients, trying out innovative recipes, and discovering the joy of eating well in a way that supports your body's needs.

## Your Path to Wellness

As you turn the pages of this cookbook, remember that each meal is an opportunity to nourish your body and support your well-being. We encourage you to embrace the journey with an open heart and a willingness to experiment. The recipes here are crafted with care to offer not just health benefits, but also the satisfaction of a well-balanced and flavorful meal. By integrating these recipes and principles into your daily life, you'll be taking significant steps towards achieving a healthier, more balanced lifestyle.

Welcome to a new chapter in your health journey. Let *The Glucose Revolution Cookbook for Beginners* be your guide to making blood sugar management both enjoyable and effective. Here's to a future where eating well is synonymous with feeling well, and where each meal brings you closer to a more vibrant and balanced life.

# Chapter 1: Understanding Blood Sugar

## 1.1   What is Blood Sugar?

Blood sugar, also referred to as blood glucose, is the amount of glucose present in your bloodstream at any given time. Glucose is a simple sugar that serves as the primary energy source for the cells in your body. It is especially crucial for brain function, as the brain depends almost exclusively on glucose for energy.

When you eat foods, particularly those containing carbohydrates, your digestive system breaks down these foods into simpler forms, including glucose. This glucose is then absorbed into your bloodstream, leading to an increase in blood sugar levels. The rise in blood sugar triggers the release of insulin, a hormone produced by the pancreas, which helps cells absorb glucose for energy or storage.

Blood sugar levels are typically measured in milligrams of glucose per deciliter of blood (mg/dL). For most healthy individuals, fasting blood sugar levels (measured after not eating for at least 8 hours) are typically between 70 and 100 mg/dL. After meals, blood sugar levels may rise, but they usually return to normal within a few hours.

Maintaining balanced blood sugar levels is crucial for overall health. If blood sugar levels are too high (a condition known as hyperglycemia) or too low (hypoglycemia), it can lead to a variety of health problems. Prolonged high blood sugar is associated with conditions like diabetes, which can have serious long-term complications such as heart disease, kidney failure, and nerve damage. On the other hand, low blood sugar can cause symptoms like dizziness, confusion, and fainting, and if severe, it can be life-threatening.

In summary, blood sugar is a critical component of your body's energy management system. Understanding what blood sugar is and how it functions is the first step in managing it effectively. By keeping your blood sugar within a healthy range, you can support your overall well-being and reduce the risk of serious health issues.

## 1.2   Knowing The Sources of Your Energy

Energy is fundamental to every function and activity in the human body, from basic processes like breathing and circulation to more complex tasks like physical exercise and mental concentration. The body derives this energy from three primary macronutrients: carbohydrates, fats, and proteins. Understanding how these nutrients contribute to energy production and affect blood sugar levels is key to managing your overall health.

### 1.2.1   Carbohydrates: The Primary Source of Glucose

Carbohydrates are the most direct source of energy for your body, as they are readily converted into glucose. When you eat carbohydrate-rich foods, such as bread, pasta, rice, fruits, and vegetables, your digestive system breaks down these foods into simple sugars, including glucose. This glucose is absorbed into the bloodstream, leading to an increase in blood sugar levels.

Carbohydrates can be classified into two main types: simple and complex. Simple carbohydrates, found in foods like sugary snacks, soft drinks, and certain fruits, are quickly digested and cause rapid spikes in blood sugar. Complex carbohydrates, found in whole grains, legumes, and starchy vegetables, are digested more slowly, leading to a gradual release of glucose and a more stable blood sugar response. For those aiming to manage their blood sugar, it is generally recommended to focus on consuming complex carbohydrates, which provide sustained energy and help prevent sharp increases in blood glucose levels.

### 1.2.2   Fats: A Long-Lasting Source of Energy

Fats are another important source of energy, but they play a different role than carbohydrates. When consumed, fats are broken down into fatty acids and glycerol, which can be used by the body for energy or stored for future use. Unlike carbohydrates, fats do not immediately raise blood sugar levels, but they are essential for providing long-lasting energy, especially during periods when carbohydrate intake is low.

Healthy fats, such as those found in avocados, nuts, seeds, and olive oil, support overall health and can help with blood sugar management by slowing the absorption of glucose. This slower absorption can prevent rapid spikes in blood sugar, contributing to more stable energy levels throughout the day. Incorporating healthy fats into your diet is a key strategy for balancing your energy sources.

### 1.2.3   Proteins: Building Blocks and a Secondary Energy Source

Proteins are primarily known for their role in building and repairing tissues, but they can also be used as a secondary source of energy, particularly when carbohydrate intake is low. When protein is consumed, it is broken down into amino acids, which are used to build and maintain muscle, skin, and other tissues. However, if the body needs energy and there is insufficient glucose available, proteins can be converted into glucose through a process called gluconeogenesis.

While proteins have a minimal immediate impact on blood sugar levels, they play a crucial role in overall energy management. High-protein foods, such as lean meats, fish, eggs, beans, and legumes, can help maintain muscle mass, support metabolic function, and provide a steady energy source. Additionally, consuming protein with carbohydrates can help moderate blood sugar spikes by slowing the digestion and absorption of glucose.

### 1.2.4   Balancing Macronutrients for Optimal Energy

Achieving a balance between carbohydrates, fats, and proteins is essential for sustaining energy levels and maintaining stable blood sugar. Each macronutrient contributes to energy production in different ways, and understanding their roles can help you make informed dietary choices that support your health goals.

A balanced diet that includes complex carbohydrates, healthy fats, and sufficient protein can provide a steady supply of energy throughout the day, prevent blood sugar fluctuations, and reduce the risk of insulin resistance and other metabolic disorders. By knowing the sources of your energy and how they interact with your body's metabolism, you can take proactive steps to manage your blood sugar and overall well-being.

## 1.3   Insulin: Role and Composition

Insulin is a hormone produced by the pancreas that plays a vital role in regulating blood sugar levels. When you consume food, particularly carbohydrates, your blood sugar levels rise, prompting your pancreas to release insulin. Insulin facilitates the uptake of glucose into cells, where it is used for energy or stored for future use. This section will explain the composition of insulin, its production in the body, and its critical role in maintaining blood sugar balance. Additionally, it will cover what happens when the body's insulin production or utilization goes awry, leading to conditions such as insulin resistance and diabetes.

## 1.4   How to Maintain a Correct Balance

Maintaining balanced blood sugar is crucial for avoiding both the short-term effects of high and low blood sugar and the long-term health complications associated with chronic imbalances. This section will provide practical tips and strategies for keeping your blood sugar within a healthy range. Topics will include the importance of regular meals, the role of fiber, the impact of exercise, and the benefits of monitoring your blood sugar levels. Additionally, it will cover lifestyle changes that can help prevent blood sugar spikes and dips.

## 1.5   The Effects of Blood Sugar on Overall Health

Blood sugar levels play a critical role in your overall health, influencing everything from energy levels to the functioning of various organ systems. Maintaining balanced blood sugar is essential not just for avoiding immediate symptoms like fatigue or dizziness, but also for preventing long-term health complications. This section will explore how blood sugar affects different aspects of health, including cardiovascular health, metabolic function, cognitive performance, and more.

### 1.5.1   Cardiovascular Health

High blood sugar levels, particularly when chronic, can have a significant impact on cardiovascular health. Elevated blood sugar can lead to the development of a condition known as insulin resistance, where the body's cells become less responsive to insulin. This, in turn, forces the pancreas to produce more insulin to manage blood glucose levels. Over time, this can lead to type 2 diabetes, which is strongly associated with an increased risk of heart disease, stroke, and other cardiovascular issues.

Excess glucose in the blood can also damage the lining of blood vessels, leading to the buildup of fatty deposits called plaques. These plaques can narrow the arteries, reduce blood flow, and increase the risk of atherosclerosis—a condition that can cause heart attacks and strokes. Furthermore, high blood sugar levels can lead to high blood pressure, another risk factor for cardiovascular disease.

### 1.5.2   Metabolic Function and Weight Management

Blood sugar levels are closely linked to metabolic health and weight management. When blood sugar levels are consistently high, the body's ability to manage glucose becomes impaired, leading to metabolic disorders such as insulin resistance and metabolic syndrome. These conditions are precursors to type 2 diabetes and are also associated with increased body fat, particularly around the abdomen, which can further exacerbate insulin resistance.

On the other hand, balanced blood sugar levels support a healthy metabolism, allowing the body to efficiently use and store energy. When glucose is properly managed, it can reduce the likelihood of unnecessary fat storage, support healthy weight management, and improve overall metabolic function. For those trying to lose weight or maintain a healthy weight, keeping blood sugar levels stable is a crucial aspect of their strategy.

### 1.5.3   Cognitive Performance and Mental Health

The brain is highly sensitive to changes in blood sugar levels, as it relies almost exclusively on glucose for energy. When blood sugar levels fluctuate widely, it can lead to cognitive impairments such as difficulty concentrating, memory problems, and mental fatigue. Low blood sugar, or hypoglycemia, can cause symptoms like dizziness, confusion, irritability, and even unconsciousness in severe cases.

Chronic high blood sugar levels have also been linked to an increased risk of cognitive decline and neurodegenerative diseases such as Alzheimer's disease. Research suggests that high blood sugar can damage brain cells and contribute to the formation of amyloid plaques, which are associated with Alzheimer's. Maintaining stable blood sugar is therefore essential not only for day-to-day cognitive performance but also for long-term brain health.

### 1.5.4 Immune System Function

Blood sugar levels also influence the functioning of the immune system. High blood sugar can suppress the immune response, making the body more susceptible to infections and slowing down the healing process. This is particularly evident in people with diabetes, who often experience slower wound healing and a higher risk of infections, including skin infections, urinary tract infections, and respiratory infections.

Conversely, well-managed blood sugar levels support a robust immune system. By keeping glucose levels within a healthy range, you can enhance your body's ability to fight off infections, recover from illnesses more quickly, and maintain overall immune resilience.

## 1.6  High Blood Sugar Explained

High blood sugar, medically known as hyperglycemia, occurs when there is an excessive amount of glucose in the bloodstream. This condition can arise from various causes, including poor dietary choices, lack of physical activity, stress, illness, or an underlying medical condition such as diabetes. Understanding the causes, symptoms, and potential consequences of high blood sugar is crucial for managing it effectively and preventing long-term health complications.

### 1.6.1  Causes of High Blood Sugar

High blood sugar can be triggered by several factors, often related to lifestyle or medical conditions:

- **Dietary Choices:** Consuming large amounts of carbohydrates, particularly simple sugars found in sweets, sugary beverages, and processed foods, can lead to rapid spikes in blood glucose levels. When the body cannot produce enough insulin, or if the insulin produced is not effective (a condition known as insulin resistance), blood sugar levels remain elevated.

- **Lack of Physical Activity:** Regular physical activity helps lower blood sugar by increasing the sensitivity of cells to insulin, allowing glucose to be used more efficiently for energy. Sedentary lifestyles contribute to higher blood sugar levels, as glucose remains in the bloodstream rather than being utilized by muscles.
- **Stress:** Both physical and emotional stress can cause the body to release hormones such as cortisol and adrenaline, which can increase blood sugar levels. These hormones trigger the liver to release stored glucose into the bloodstream as part of the "fight or flight" response.
- **Illness:** During illness or infection, the body's stress response can lead to increased blood sugar levels. This is particularly concerning for people with diabetes, as managing blood sugar during illness can be more challenging.
- **Medical Conditions:** The most common cause of chronic high blood sugar is diabetes, particularly type 1 and type 2 diabetes. In type 1 diabetes, the body's immune system attacks the insulin-producing cells in the pancreas, leading to a lack of insulin. In type 2 diabetes, the body either doesn't produce enough insulin or becomes resistant to its effects, resulting in elevated blood sugar levels.

## 1.6.2   Symptoms of High Blood Sugar

Recognizing the symptoms of high blood sugar is important for timely intervention. Common symptoms include:

- **Frequent Urination:** Excess glucose in the blood is filtered out by the kidneys and excreted in urine, leading to increased urination. This can also cause dehydration if fluid intake does not keep up with the loss.
- **Increased Thirst:** As a result of dehydration from frequent urination, individuals often experience excessive thirst, a condition known as polydipsia.
- **Fatigue:** When glucose cannot enter the cells to be used for energy, the body may feel fatigued and weak, as cells are essentially starved of their primary fuel source.
- **Blurred Vision:** High blood sugar can cause the lenses of the eyes to swell, leading to temporary changes in vision and blurriness.
- **Headaches:** High blood sugar levels can lead to headaches due to dehydration and changes in blood vessels.
- **Slow Wound Healing:** High blood sugar levels can impair blood circulation and damage nerves, leading to slower healing of cuts, sores, and infections.
- **Weight Loss:** In some cases, especially in type 1 diabetes, high blood sugar can lead to unintentional weight loss as the body starts to break down fat and muscle for energy when it cannot access glucose.

## 1.6.3   Prevention and Management of High Blood Sugar

Preventing and managing high blood sugar is essential for overall health and well-being. Strategies include:

- **Dietary Modifications:** Focus on a balanced diet rich in whole grains, vegetables, lean proteins, and healthy fats. Limiting the intake of refined sugars and processed foods can help prevent spikes in blood sugar.
- **Regular Exercise:** Physical activity helps improve insulin sensitivity, allowing cells to use glucose more effectively. Regular exercise also helps manage weight, which is crucial for controlling blood sugar.
- **Medications:** For individuals with diabetes, medications such as insulin or oral hypoglycemic agents may be necessary to manage blood sugar levels. It's important to follow prescribed treatment plans and monitor blood sugar regularly.
- **Stress Management:** Reducing stress through techniques like meditation, deep breathing, and regular physical activity can help lower cortisol levels and prevent stress-induced blood sugar spikes.
- **Regular Monitoring:** For those at risk of high blood sugar, regular monitoring through blood glucose tests can help detect and manage hyperglycemia before it leads to serious complications.

## 1.7  Low Blood Sugar Explained

Low blood sugar, also known as hypoglycemia, occurs when the level of glucose in your blood falls below the normal range. For most people, this threshold is generally considered to be below 70 mg/dL, although the specific level at which symptoms appear can vary from person to person. Hypoglycemia is a condition that requires prompt attention, as it can lead to serious health consequences if not managed effectively. This section will explore the causes, symptoms, and potential risks associated with low blood sugar, as well as strategies for prevention and treatment.

### 1.7.1  Causes of Low Blood Sugar

Low blood sugar can result from a variety of factors, many of which are related to medication, diet, and lifestyle. Some of the most common causes include:

- **Diabetes Medications:** For people with diabetes, particularly those taking insulin or other medications that increase insulin production, low blood sugar is a common risk. These medications lower blood sugar by helping glucose move into cells, but if too much insulin is present, or if the person skips a meal, blood sugar can drop too low.
- **Skipping Meals or Eating Too Little:** Not eating enough food or delaying meals can lead to low blood sugar, especially in individuals who have diabetes or are sensitive to changes in blood glucose levels. When the body does not receive a steady supply of glucose from food, it can lead to hypoglycemia.
- **Intense Physical Activity:** Engaging in vigorous exercise without properly adjusting food intake or insulin dosage can cause blood sugar to drop. Exercise uses up glucose stored in muscles and the liver, and if this glucose is not

replenished, hypoglycemia can occur.

- **Alcohol Consumption:** Drinking alcohol, especially on an empty stomach, can interfere with the liver's ability to release glucose into the bloodstream, leading to hypoglycemia. This effect can be particularly dangerous because the symptoms of low blood sugar can be mistaken for intoxication.
- **Certain Medical Conditions:** Some medical conditions, such as adrenal insufficiency, liver disease, or severe infections, can cause hypoglycemia. These conditions may affect the body's ability to regulate blood sugar or deplete glucose stores.
- **Reactive Hypoglycemia:** In some individuals, eating a large amount of carbohydrates can cause an excessive release of insulin, leading to a rapid drop in blood sugar levels after the meal. This condition is known as reactive hypoglycemia.

## 1.7.2   Symptoms of Low Blood Sugar

The symptoms of low blood sugar can vary in severity, ranging from mild discomfort to serious medical emergencies. Common symptoms include:

- **Shakiness and Trembling:** One of the most common early signs of hypoglycemia is a feeling of shakiness or trembling, as the body reacts to low glucose levels by releasing adrenaline.
- **Sweating:** Excessive sweating, especially cold sweats, can occur as the body attempts to correct the imbalance in blood sugar.
- **Hunger:** Intense hunger, often accompanied by feelings of irritability (sometimes called "hangry"), is a common symptom as the body signals the need for more glucose.
- **Dizziness and Lightheadedness:** Low blood sugar can cause dizziness, lightheadedness, and difficulty maintaining balance, making it hard to perform daily activities safely.
- **Confusion and Difficulty Concentrating:** The brain relies heavily on glucose for energy, so when blood sugar drops, cognitive functions can become impaired. This can manifest as confusion, difficulty concentrating, or even slurred speech.
- **Blurred Vision:** Similar to high blood sugar, low blood sugar can also affect vision, causing blurriness or double vision.
- **Weakness and Fatigue:** As the body's cells are deprived of glucose, general weakness and fatigue can set in, making it difficult to move or stay awake.
- **Rapid Heartbeat:** Hypoglycemia can cause an increase in heart rate, often felt as palpitations or a racing heartbeat.
- **Severe Symptoms:** If blood sugar levels continue to drop and are not addressed, more severe symptoms can develop, including seizures, loss of consciousness, and in extreme cases, coma or death. These severe symptoms require immediate medical intervention.

### 1.7.3  Prevention and Management of Low Blood Sugar

Preventing and managing low blood sugar is essential for maintaining overall health and quality of life. Strategies include:

- **Regular Monitoring:** For people at risk of hypoglycemia, regular monitoring of blood sugar levels is crucial. This can help detect low levels before symptoms become severe and allow for timely intervention.
- **Balanced Diet:** Eating regular, balanced meals that include a mix of carbohydrates, proteins, and fats can help maintain stable blood sugar levels. It's also important to avoid skipping meals, especially if taking medications that lower blood sugar.
- **Adjusting Medications:** For those on diabetes medications, it may be necessary to adjust dosages or timing to prevent low blood sugar. This should always be done under the guidance of a healthcare provider.
- **Carrying Fast-Acting Carbohydrates:** Individuals prone to hypoglycemia should always carry a source of fast-acting carbohydrates, such as glucose tablets, candy, or juice, to quickly raise blood sugar levels if they begin to drop.
- **Educating Friends and Family:** Educating those around you about the signs of hypoglycemia and how to respond can ensure that help is available if needed.
- **Alcohol and Exercise Precautions:** If consuming alcohol or engaging in strenuous exercise, it's important to take precautions such as eating a snack beforehand, monitoring blood sugar closely, and being aware of the delayed effects these activities can have on glucose levels.

## 1.8   Balanced Diet for Blood Sugar Management

A balanced diet is fundamental in managing blood sugar levels and promoting overall health. It involves consuming a variety of nutrients in the right proportions to support stable glucose levels and prevent both high and low blood sugar. This section highlights the importance of dietary balance and provides key strategies for maintaining optimal blood sugar control.

### 1.8.1   Importance of a Balanced Diet

Maintaining a balanced diet is crucial for blood sugar management due to the following reasons:

- **Stable Blood Sugar Levels:** A balanced diet helps regulate the release of glucose into the bloodstream, preventing sharp spikes and drops in blood sugar. This stability is vital for individuals with diabetes and those at risk of glucose imbalances.
- **Improved Insulin Sensitivity:** Consuming a mix of nutrients, including fiber, proteins, and healthy fats, can enhance insulin sensitivity. This means the body uses insulin more effectively, aiding in better blood sugar control.

- **Reduced Risk of Complications:** Proper dietary management can reduce the risk of developing complications associated with poorly managed blood sugar, such as cardiovascular disease, nerve damage, and kidney issues.
- **Overall Health Benefits:** A balanced diet not only supports blood sugar control but also contributes to overall health, including weight management, cardiovascular health, and improved energy levels.

## 1.8.2   Key Components of a Blood Sugar-Friendly Diet

To maintain a balanced diet for blood sugar management, consider the following components:

- **Complex Carbohydrates:** Choose whole grains, legumes, and starchy vegetables over refined carbohydrates. These foods release glucose gradually and help maintain steady blood sugar levels.
- **Fiber-Rich Foods:** Incorporate fruits, vegetables, and whole grains into your diet. Fiber slows the absorption of glucose, which helps prevent rapid blood sugar spikes.
- **Lean Proteins and Healthy Fats:** Include sources of lean protein and healthy fats, such as fish, poultry, nuts, and avocados. These components help keep you full and can aid in better blood sugar control.
- **Moderation and Portion Control:** Pay attention to portion sizes and avoid overeating. Balancing portions helps manage calorie intake and prevents excessive glucose load.

## 1.8.3   Practical Tips for Implementation

- **Plan Balanced Meals:** Aim to include a mix of carbohydrates, proteins, and fats in each meal. This balance helps stabilize blood sugar levels and supports sustained energy.
- **Monitor Blood Sugar:** Regular monitoring of blood sugar levels can provide insights into how different foods affect your glucose levels, allowing for better dietary adjustments.
- **Stay Hydrated:** Drink plenty of water throughout the day, as proper hydration supports metabolic processes and overall health.

# Chapter 2: Balancing Blood Sugar for Optimal Hormone Health and Metabolism

## 2.1 Insulin and Blood Sugar Regulation

Insulin is a crucial hormone produced by the pancreas that plays a central role in regulating blood sugar levels. It facilitates the uptake of glucose into cells, helping to maintain normal blood glucose levels and ensuring that the body's energy needs are met. This section delves into the mechanisms by which insulin regulates blood sugar, the effects of insulin resistance, and the impact of insulin on overall metabolic health.

### 2.1.1 The Role of Insulin in Blood Sugar Regulation

Insulin is produced by beta cells in the pancreas and is released into the bloodstream in response to elevated blood glucose levels, such as after eating a meal:

- **Glucose Uptake:** Insulin promotes the uptake of glucose into cells, particularly muscle and fat cells, by binding to insulin receptors on the cell membrane. This binding activates a series of intracellular processes that allow glucose to enter the cell, where it can be used for energy or stored for later use.
- **Glycogen Storage:** In the liver and muscles, insulin facilitates the conversion of excess glucose into glycogen, a storage form of glucose. This stored glycogen can be broken down and released into the bloodstream when blood glucose levels are low, such as between meals or during physical activity.
- **Inhibition of Gluconeogenesis:** Insulin inhibits gluconeogenesis, the process by which the liver produces new glucose from non-carbohydrate sources. By suppressing this process, insulin helps to lower blood glucose levels after eating.

### 2.1.2 Insulin Resistance and Its Effects

Insulin resistance occurs when the body's cells become less responsive to insulin, leading to impaired glucose uptake and elevated blood sugar levels. This condition is a hallmark of type 2 diabetes and metabolic syndrome:

- **Mechanisms of Insulin Resistance:** Insulin resistance can develop due to various factors, including genetic predisposition, obesity, and physical inactivity.

In insulin resistance, the insulin receptors on cells become less effective at binding insulin, or the signaling pathways within the cells are impaired, leading to reduced glucose uptake.

- **Compensatory Hyperinsulinemia:** To overcome insulin resistance, the pancreas produces more insulin, a condition known as hyperinsulinemia. Elevated insulin levels are an attempt to maintain normal blood glucose levels despite reduced cellular response.
- **Impact on Metabolic Health:** Chronic insulin resistance can lead to higher levels of circulating glucose and insulin, contributing to the development of type 2 diabetes, cardiovascular disease, and other metabolic disorders. Insulin resistance is also associated with increased fat accumulation, particularly in the abdominal area, which further exacerbates metabolic issues.

### 2.1.3   Regulating Insulin and Blood Sugar Levels

Effective management of insulin and blood sugar levels involves lifestyle changes and, in some cases, medical interventions:

- **Dietary Choices:** Consuming a balanced diet with a focus on low glycemic index foods, fiber-rich carbohydrates, lean proteins, and healthy fats can help regulate blood sugar levels and improve insulin sensitivity. Avoiding excessive sugar and refined carbohydrates is crucial for managing insulin levels.
- **Physical Activity:** Regular exercise enhances insulin sensitivity by increasing glucose uptake by muscles and improving overall metabolic health. Both aerobic exercise and resistance training are beneficial for maintaining healthy blood sugar levels.
- **Weight Management:** Maintaining a healthy weight or losing excess weight can improve insulin sensitivity and reduce the risk of insulin resistance. Weight loss can help lower circulating levels of insulin and glucose, improving overall blood sugar control.
- **Medical Management:** For individuals with insulin resistance or type 2 diabetes, medications such as metformin or insulin therapy may be prescribed to help manage blood glucose levels. These treatments work by enhancing insulin sensitivity, reducing glucose production, or increasing insulin availability.

### 2.1.4   The Interplay Between Insulin and Other Hormones

Insulin interacts with other hormones that influence blood sugar regulation:

- **Glucagon:** Produced by the alpha cells of the pancreas, glucagon works in opposition to insulin. It stimulates the release of glucose from glycogen stores in the liver and promotes gluconeogenesis, helping to raise blood sugar levels when they are low.
- **Cortisol:** This stress hormone, produced by the adrenal glands, can increase blood glucose levels by promoting gluconeogenesis and reducing insulin

sensitivity. Chronic stress and elevated cortisol levels can exacerbate insulin resistance.

- **Epinephrine:** Also known as adrenaline, epinephrine is released during the "fight or flight" response. It increases blood glucose levels by stimulating glycogen breakdown and glucose release from the liver.

## 2.2 Cortisol and Its Effects on Stress Management

Cortisol is a steroid hormone produced by the adrenal glands in response to stress. Often referred to as the "stress hormone," cortisol plays a crucial role in the body's fight-or-flight response, regulating various physiological processes to help manage stress. This section explores the role of cortisol in stress management, its effects on the body, and strategies for maintaining healthy cortisol levels.

### 2.2.1 Role of Cortisol in the Stress Response

Cortisol is released in response to acute or chronic stress, preparing the body to handle challenging situations:

- **Activation of the Hypothalamic-Pituitary-Adrenal (HPA) Axis:** Stress activates the HPA axis, a complex set of interactions between the hypothalamus, pituitary gland, and adrenal glands. In response to stress, the hypothalamus releases corticotropin-releasing hormone (CRH), which stimulates the pituitary gland to secrete adrenocorticotropic hormone (ACTH). ACTH then prompts the adrenal glands to produce and release cortisol.
- **Energy Mobilization:** Cortisol helps mobilize energy by stimulating the breakdown of glycogen in the liver and promoting gluconeogenesis, the production of new glucose. This ensures that glucose is available for immediate use by muscles and other vital organs during stressful situations.
- **Anti-Inflammatory Effects:** Cortisol has anti-inflammatory properties that help regulate the immune response and prevent excessive inflammation. This is beneficial in managing acute stress but can be detrimental if cortisol levels remain elevated for extended periods.

### 2.2.2 Effects of Elevated Cortisol Levels

While cortisol is essential for managing short-term stress, chronic elevation of cortisol levels can have several negative effects on health:

- **Impact on Metabolism:** Prolonged high cortisol levels can lead to increased appetite and cravings for high-calorie foods, contributing to weight gain, particularly around the abdominal area. Elevated cortisol also affects insulin sensitivity, increasing the risk of insulin resistance and type 2 diabetes.

- **Immune System Suppression:** Chronic cortisol elevation can suppress the immune system, making the body more susceptible to infections and delaying the healing process. This occurs because prolonged cortisol exposure inhibits the production of inflammatory cytokines and reduces immune cell activity.
- **Cardiovascular Health:** Elevated cortisol levels can contribute to hypertension (high blood pressure) and increase the risk of cardiovascular disease. Cortisol promotes the retention of sodium and water, leading to increased blood volume and pressure.
- **Cognitive Function and Mood:** Long-term stress and high cortisol levels can negatively affect cognitive functions such as memory and concentration. It can also contribute to mood disorders, including anxiety and depression, due to its impact on neurotransmitter systems and brain function.
- **Sleep Disruption:** High cortisol levels, especially in the evening, can interfere with sleep patterns, making it difficult to fall asleep and stay asleep. Poor sleep quality can exacerbate stress and create a vicious cycle of elevated cortisol and disrupted sleep.

## 2.2.3   Strategies for Managing Cortisol Levels

Effective stress management involves strategies to regulate cortisol levels and promote overall well-being:

- **Regular Physical Activity:** Engaging in regular exercise helps reduce cortisol levels and improve overall stress resilience. Both aerobic exercises (such as walking, running, and swimming) and mind-body practices (like yoga and tai chi) can be effective.
- **Healthy Diet:** Consuming a balanced diet rich in whole foods, including fruits, vegetables, lean proteins, and whole grains, supports overall health and helps manage cortisol levels. Reducing the intake of caffeine, sugar, and processed foods can also help lower cortisol.
- **Adequate Sleep:** Prioritizing good sleep hygiene and ensuring 7-9 hours of quality sleep per night is crucial for maintaining healthy cortisol levels. Consistent sleep schedules, a comfortable sleep environment, and relaxation techniques can improve sleep quality.
- **Stress Management Techniques:** Incorporating stress management practices such as mindfulness meditation, deep breathing exercises, and progressive muscle relaxation can help lower cortisol levels and improve emotional resilience.
- **Social Support:** Building and maintaining strong social connections provides emotional support and helps buffer the effects of stress. Engaging in social activities and seeking support from friends, family, or a therapist can be beneficial.
- **Time Management:** Effective time management and setting realistic goals can reduce stress by preventing feelings of overwhelm and ensuring a balanced approach to work and personal life.

### 2.2.4  When to Seek Professional Help

If chronic stress and elevated cortisol levels are impacting your health and well-being, it may be beneficial to seek professional help. Healthcare providers can assess cortisol levels, provide guidance on managing stress, and offer treatments for related health conditions. In some cases, medications or therapy may be necessary to address persistent issues.

## 2.3  How Blood Sugar Influences Estrogen and Progesterone

Blood sugar levels can significantly impact hormonal balance, including the hormones estrogen and progesterone. These two hormones are critical for reproductive health, menstrual cycle regulation, and overall hormonal equilibrium. This section explores the ways in which fluctuations in blood sugar can affect estrogen and progesterone levels, and the implications for health.

### 2.3.1  The Relationship Between Blood Sugar and Hormonal Balance

**Blood Sugar Regulation and Hormone Production**

Maintaining stable blood sugar levels is essential for the proper functioning of the endocrine system, which includes the production and regulation of hormones like estrogen and progesterone:

- **Insulin and Hormone Synthesis:** Insulin, a hormone that regulates blood sugar levels, also influences the production and metabolism of other hormones. Insulin resistance or elevated blood sugar levels can disrupt the balance of estrogen and progesterone by affecting the enzymes involved in their synthesis.
- **Glycemic Control and Hormone Conversion:** Stable blood sugar levels help ensure the proper conversion of hormones. For instance, the balance between estrogen and progesterone is partially regulated by their conversion processes in the liver, which can be influenced by blood sugar and insulin levels.

### 2.3.2  Effects of Blood Sugar Imbalance on Estrogen Levels

Estrogen is a key hormone in both men and women, involved in regulating reproductive functions and maintaining bone density. Blood sugar imbalances can affect estrogen levels in several ways:

- **Estrogen Dominance:** Chronic high blood sugar and insulin resistance can lead to increased levels of circulating estrogen, a condition known as estrogen dominance. This occurs because insulin resistance often causes higher levels of circulating insulin, which can increase estrogen production by stimulating the ovaries or by affecting estrogen metabolism in the liver.

- **Impact on Menstrual Cycle:** Fluctuations in blood sugar can lead to irregular menstrual cycles and symptoms of premenstrual syndrome (PMS). Elevated blood sugar can exacerbate symptoms such as mood swings, bloating, and irritability by disrupting the balance of estrogen.
- **Increased Risk of Estrogen-Related Conditions:** High blood sugar and insulin resistance can increase the risk of estrogen-related conditions, such as polycystic ovary syndrome (PCOS) and endometriosis. These conditions are characterized by an imbalance in estrogen levels and can be worsened by poor blood sugar control.

### 2.3.3 Effects of Blood Sugar Imbalance on Progesterone Levels

Progesterone is another crucial hormone involved in regulating the menstrual cycle and supporting pregnancy. Imbalances in blood sugar can affect progesterone levels in various ways:

- **Progesterone Deficiency:** Chronic high blood sugar can lead to lower levels of progesterone. Insulin resistance and elevated blood glucose can interfere with the body's ability to produce adequate progesterone, leading to symptoms such as irregular periods, infertility, and increased risk of miscarriage.
- **Impact on Luteal Phase:** The luteal phase of the menstrual cycle, which is when progesterone levels are naturally higher, can be disrupted by poor blood sugar control. Low progesterone levels can result in a shortened luteal phase, leading to symptoms of PMS and difficulties with conception.
- **Hormone Interactions:** Blood sugar imbalances can affect the interaction between progesterone and other hormones. For instance, elevated estrogen levels due to high blood sugar can further disrupt progesterone balance, exacerbating symptoms and health issues related to hormonal imbalances.

## 2.4 Testosterone and Its Functions

Testosterone is a key hormone in both men and women, though it is typically present at higher levels in men. It plays a crucial role in various physiological processes, including reproductive health, muscle mass maintenance, and overall vitality.

### 2.4.1 Role of Testosterone

- **Reproductive Health:** In men, testosterone is essential for the development of male reproductive tissues, including the testes and prostate. It also regulates sperm production and libido. In women, testosterone contributes to ovarian function and overall sexual health.
- **Muscle Mass and Strength:** Testosterone supports muscle growth and maintenance. It enhances protein synthesis, which helps build and repair muscle tissue, contributing to overall strength and physical performance.

- **Bone Density:** Testosterone plays a role in maintaining bone density by influencing bone mineralization and reducing the risk of osteoporosis. Both men and women require adequate testosterone levels to support healthy bones.
- **Mood and Cognitive Function:** Adequate levels of testosterone are linked to improved mood, cognitive function, and overall mental well-being. Low testosterone levels can contribute to symptoms of depression, fatigue, and difficulty concentrating.

### 2.4.2 Impact of Blood Sugar Imbalance on Testosterone

- **Insulin Resistance:** High blood sugar and insulin resistance can lead to reduced testosterone levels. Insulin resistance can interfere with the production and function of testosterone, contributing to symptoms such as decreased libido and reduced muscle mass.
- **Chronic Stress:** Elevated cortisol levels from chronic stress can lower testosterone levels. Cortisol and testosterone have a balancing effect; when cortisol is high, it can suppress testosterone production.
- **Weight Gain:** Excessive weight and obesity can negatively affect testosterone levels. Higher levels of body fat, particularly abdominal fat, are associated with lower testosterone levels and increased aromatization of testosterone to estrogen.

### 2.4.3 Maintaining Healthy Testosterone Levels

- **Balanced Diet:** Consume a diet rich in essential nutrients, including healthy fats, proteins, and vitamins, to support testosterone production. Avoid excessive sugar and refined carbs that can disrupt blood sugar balance.
- **Regular Exercise:** Engage in regular physical activity, including strength training and aerobic exercise, to boost testosterone levels and improve overall metabolic health.
- **Stress Management:** Implement stress-reducing practices such as mindfulness and relaxation techniques to help maintain balanced cortisol and testosterone levels.
- **Adequate Sleep:** Ensure sufficient, quality sleep to support hormone production and overall health. Aim for 7-9 hours of restful sleep per night.

## 2.5 How to Balance Blood Sugar with Ease

Balancing blood sugar is crucial for maintaining overall health, energy levels, and preventing chronic conditions such as diabetes. Implementing simple yet effective strategies can help stabilize blood sugar levels and support long-term well-being. This section outlines practical tips and lifestyle changes for achieving balanced blood sugar with ease so it will be sustainable for you in the long run!

### 2.5.1  Adopt a Balanced Diet

- **Incorporate Complex Carbohydrates:** Choose whole grains, legumes, and starchy vegetables over refined carbohydrates. Complex carbohydrates release glucose slowly into the bloodstream, preventing rapid spikes and dips.
- **Include Fiber-Rich Foods:** Foods high in dietary fiber, such as fruits, vegetables, and whole grains, help slow the absorption of glucose. Fiber also promotes satiety, reducing the likelihood of overeating and stabilizing blood sugar levels.
- **Opt for Lean Proteins and Healthy Fats:** Incorporate sources of lean protein (e.g., chicken, fish, tofu) and healthy fats (e.g., avocados, nuts) into your meals. These macronutrients help stabilize blood sugar by slowing the digestion of carbohydrates and promoting balanced energy levels.

### 2.5.2  Monitor Portion Sizes

- **Practice Portion Control:** Eating appropriate portion sizes helps prevent excessive calorie intake and maintains steady blood sugar levels. Use smaller plates, measure servings, and be mindful of portion sizes to avoid overeating.
- **Balanced Meals:** Aim to include a balance of carbohydrates, proteins, and fats in each meal. This combination helps slow glucose absorption and promotes sustained energy throughout the day.

### 2.5.3  Regular Physical Activity

- **Engage in Aerobic Exercise:** Activities such as walking, running, and swimming help improve insulin sensitivity and aid in blood sugar regulation. Aim for at least 150 minutes of moderate-intensity aerobic exercise per week.
- **Incorporate Strength Training:** Resistance exercises, such as lifting weights or bodyweight exercises, build muscle mass and enhance glucose uptake by cells. Include strength training exercises at least twice a week.

### 2.5.4  Manage Stress Effectively

- **Practice Stress Reduction Techniques:** Incorporate mindfulness, meditation, and deep breathing exercises to manage stress levels. Chronic stress can negatively impact blood sugar control by increasing cortisol levels.
- **Engage in Relaxing Activities:** Spend time on activities that you enjoy and that help you relax, such as hobbies, spending time with loved ones, or taking nature walks. Reducing stress helps support balanced blood sugar levels.

# Chapter 3: Delicious and Nutritious Breakfasts for Balancing Blood Sugar

Managing blood sugar levels can seem overwhelming, filled with concerns about the future and apprehensions about how our dietary choices impact our health. However, it's important to remember that every journey begins with a single step, and every meal is an opportunity for balance and renewal. In this chapter, we invite you to explore a variety of delicious and nutritious breakfast options designed specifically to support blood sugar stability and nourish your body from the inside out. From wholesome oatmeal bowls topped with fiber-rich fruits to savory egg dishes packed with essential nutrients, each recipe is thoughtfully crafted to provide the sustenance you need to maintain balanced blood sugar levels.

As you navigate these pages, remember that your current state does not define your entire journey. While managing blood sugar may be a significant part of your life, it is just one chapter in your broader story. You have the power to take control of your health, one meal at a time, and make choices that enhance your well-being. Embrace this journey with an open mind and a zest for new flavors, allowing yourself to enjoy the pleasures of eating well even as you tackle the challenges of blood sugar management. Healing and balance are not always linear—they involve a series of adjustments, setbacks, and triumphs. With patience, persistence, and a bit of culinary creativity, you can move toward a healthier, more vibrant future.

So, as you embark on this culinary exploration, set aside your worries and embrace the opportunities that lie ahead. Let each meal be a celebration of your commitment to balanced living and a testament to your resilience. Together, let us nourish our bodies, uplift our spirits, and rediscover the joy of balanced eating. In the kitchen, as in life, there is always space for hope, balance, and the simple pleasures that make each day worth savoring.

## 3.1 Mediterranean Quinoa Salad with Lemon-Herb Dressing

**Ingredients:**

- 185 grams quinoa, rinsed
- 475 milliliters water or vegetable broth
- 150 grams cherry tomatoes, halved
- 1 cucumber, diced
- 1/2 red onion, finely chopped
- 75 grams Kalamata olives, pitted and sliced
- 75 grams crumbled feta cheese (optional)
- 15 grams chopped fresh parsley
- 15 grams chopped fresh mint
- Salt and pepper to taste

**Instructions:**

1. In a medium saucepan, combine the quinoa and water or vegetable broth. Bring to a boil, then reduce the heat to low, cover, and simmer for 15-20 minutes, or until the quinoa is tender and the liquid is absorbed. Remove from heat and let it cool slightly.

2. In a large bowl, combine the cooked quinoa, cherry tomatoes, cucumber, red onion, Kalamata olives, feta cheese (if using), parsley, and mint. Toss gently to combine.

3. In a small bowl, whisk together the extra virgin olive oil, lemon juice, lemon zest, minced garlic, Dijon mustard, honey or maple syrup (if using), chopped parsley, and chopped mint until well combined. Season with salt and pepper to taste.

4. Pour the lemon-herb dressing over the quinoa salad and toss until evenly coated.

5. Taste and adjust seasoning if necessary. You can add more lemon juice or olive oil if desired.

6. Serve the Mediterranean quinoa salad immediately or refrigerate for at least 30 minutes to allow the flavors to meld together before serving. Enjoy!

## 3.2  Roasted Vegetable Frittata with Spinach and Feta

**Ingredients:**

- 8 large eggs
- 1/4 cup milk or non-dairy milk alternative
- 1 tablespoon olive oil
- 1 small red onion, diced
- 1 bell pepper, diced
- 1 zucchini, diced
- 1 cup cherry tomatoes, halved
- 2 cups fresh spinach leaves
- 1/2 cup crumbled feta cheese
- Salt and pepper to taste

**Instructions:**

1. Preheat your oven to 375°F (190°C). Lightly grease a 9-inch oven-safe skillet or baking dish with olive oil or cooking spray.

2. Place the eggs and milk in a mixing bowl and whisk until well combined. Season with salt and pepper to taste. Set aside.

3. Heat the olive oil in a skillet over medium heat. Add the diced red onion and bell pepper, and sauté for 2-3 minutes, or until softened.

4. Add the diced zucchini to the skillet and cook for an additional 2-3 minutes, or until slightly tender.

5. Stir in the cherry tomatoes and fresh spinach leaves, and cook for another 1-2 minutes, or until the spinach wilts slightly.

6. Pour the egg mixture over the roasted vegetables in the skillet. Sprinkle the crumbled feta cheese evenly over the top.

7. Transfer the skillet to the preheated oven and bake for 20-25 minutes, or until the frittata is set in the center and the edges are golden brown.

8. Once cooked, remove the frittata from the oven and let it cool slightly for a few minutes.

9. Slice the roasted vegetable frittata into wedges and serve warm.

Enjoy this delicious and nutritious Roasted Vegetable Frittata with Spinach and Feta for a satisfying breakfast or brunch!

## 3.3   Lemon-Garlic Shrimp Skewers with Herbed Quinoa

**Ingredients:**

- 500 grams large shrimp, peeled and deveined
- 3 cloves garlic, minced
- Zest and juice of 1 lemon
- 2 tablespoons olive oil
- 1 tablespoon chopped fresh parsley
- Salt and pepper to taste
- 1 cup quinoa
- 2 cups water or vegetable broth
- 1 tablespoon chopped fresh basil
- 1 tablespoon chopped fresh cilantro

**Instructions:**

1. In a large bowl, combine the shrimp, minced garlic, lemon zest, lemon juice, olive oil, chopped parsley, salt, and pepper. Toss until the shrimp are evenly coated. Cover and refrigerate for at least 30 minutes to marinate.

2. Meanwhile, rinse the quinoa under cold water. In a medium saucepan, combine the quinoa and water or vegetable broth. Bring to a boil, then reduce the heat to low, cover, and simmer for 15-20 minutes, or until the quinoa is tender and the liquid is absorbed. Remove from heat and let it sit, covered, for 5 minutes. Fluff the quinoa with a fork and stir in the chopped basil and cilantro.

3. Preheat your grill or grill pan to medium-high heat. Thread the marinated shrimp onto skewers, leaving a small space between each shrimp.

4. Grill the shrimp skewers for 2-3 minutes per side, or until they are pink and opaque.

5. Serve the lemon-garlic shrimp skewers hot, alongside the herbed quinoa. Enjoy!

## 3.4   Grilled Veggie Quesadillas with Guacamole

**Ingredients:**

- 2 large flour tortillas
- 1 cup shredded Monterey Jack cheese
- 1 cup mixed grilled vegetables (such as bell peppers, zucchini, and mushrooms), diced
- 1/2 cup black beans, drained and rinsed
- 1/4 cup chopped fresh cilantro
- 1 avocado, peeled, pitted, and mashed
- 1 tablespoon lime juice
- 1 clove garlic, minced
- Salt and pepper to taste
- Olive oil or cooking spray, for grilling

**Instructions:**

1. In a small bowl, mix together the mashed avocado, lime juice, minced garlic, chopped cilantro, salt, and pepper to make the guacamole. Set aside.

2. Heat a grill pan or skillet over medium heat. Brush one side of each tortilla lightly with olive oil or spray with cooking spray.

3. Place one tortilla, oiled side down, on the grill pan. Sprinkle half of the shredded Monterey Jack cheese evenly over the tortilla.

4. Arrange the mixed grilled vegetables and black beans over the cheese.

5. Sprinkle the remaining cheese over the vegetables and beans. Top with the second tortilla, oiled side up.

6. Cook the quesadilla for 3-4 minutes on each side, or until the tortilla is golden brown and the cheese is melted.

7. Remove the quesadilla from the grill pan and let it cool slightly before slicing into wedges.

8. Serve the grilled veggie quesadillas hot, with a dollop of guacamole on top. Enjoy!

## 3.5 Avocado Toast with Poached Eggs and Cherry Tomatoes

**Ingredients:**

- 2 slices whole grain bread
- 200 grams cherry tomatoes, halved
- 2 ripe avocados
- 4 large eggs
- 2 teaspoons white vinegar
- Salt and pepper to taste
- Optional toppings: red pepper flakes, chopped chives, or crumbled feta cheese

**Instructions:**

1. Fill a medium saucepan with water and bring it to a gentle simmer over medium heat. Add the white vinegar to the water.

2. Crack one egg into a small bowl or ramekin. Using a spoon, create a gentle whirlpool in the simmering water. Carefully slide the egg into the center of the whirlpool. Repeat with the remaining eggs, one at a time. Poach the eggs for 3-4 minutes, or until the whites are set but the yolks are still runny. Use a slotted spoon to remove the poached eggs from the water and transfer them to a plate lined with paper towels to drain.

3. While the eggs are poaching, toast the bread slices until golden brown.

4. Mash the ripe avocados in a small bowl with a fork. Season with salt and pepper to taste.

5. Spread the mashed avocado evenly onto the toasted bread slices.

6. Top each avocado toast with halved cherry tomatoes and a poached egg.

7. Garnish with optional toppings such as red pepper flakes, chopped chives, or crumbled feta cheese, if desired.

8. Serve the avocado toast with poached eggs and cherry tomatoes immediately. Enjoy!

## 3.6   Spinach and Mushroom Omelette with Goat Cheese

**Ingredients:**

- 4 large eggs
- 50 grams baby spinach leaves
- 100 grams mushrooms, sliced
- 50 grams goat cheese, crumbled
- 1 tablespoon olive oil
- Salt and pepper to taste

**Instructions:**

1. In a mixing bowl, whisk the eggs until well beaten. Season with salt and pepper to taste.

2. Heat the olive oil in a non-stick skillet over medium heat. Add the sliced mushrooms and sauté for 2-3 minutes, or until they are golden brown and tender.

3. Add the baby spinach leaves to the skillet and cook for another 1-2 minutes, or until wilted.

4. Pour the beaten eggs over the mushrooms and spinach in the skillet. Allow the eggs to cook undisturbed for a few minutes, until the edges begin to set.

5. Using a spatula, gently lift the edges of the omelette and tilt the skillet to allow the uncooked eggs to flow underneath.

6. Once the omelette is mostly set but still slightly runny on top, sprinkle the crumbled goat cheese evenly over one half of the omelette.

7. Carefully fold the other half of the omelette over the goat cheese to create a half-moon shape. Press down gently with the spatula to seal.

8. Cook the omelette for another 1-2 minutes, or until the cheese is melted and the eggs are cooked through.

9. Slide the spinach and mushroom omelette onto a plate and serve hot. Enjoy!

## 3.7 Banana Nut Overnight Oats

**Ingredients:**

- 1 ripe banana, mashed (about 120 grams)
- 50 grams rolled oats
- 120 milliliters almond milk or any milk of your choice
- 15 grams chia seeds
- 15 grams maple syrup or honey
- 30 grams chopped nuts (such as walnuts, almonds, or pecans)
- 1/4 teaspoon vanilla extract
- Pinch of cinnamon

**Instructions:**

1. In a jar or airtight container, combine the mashed banana, rolled oats, almond milk, chia seeds, maple syrup or honey, chopped nuts, vanilla extract, and pinch of cinnamon. Stir well to combine.

2. Cover the jar or container and refrigerate overnight, or for at least 4 hours, to allow the oats to soften and absorb the liquid.

3. In the morning, give the overnight oats a stir and add a splash of additional milk if desired to reach your preferred consistency.

4. Serve the banana nut overnight oats cold, topped with extra chopped nuts or sliced banana if desired. Enjoy!

## 3.8   Blueberry Almond Smoothie Bowl

**Ingredients:**

- 150 grams frozen blueberries
- 1 ripe banana, sliced (about 120 grams)
- 120 milliliters almond milk or any milk of your choice
- 30 grams rolled oats
- 15 grams almond butter
- 1 tablespoon honey or maple syrup
- 1 tablespoon chia seeds
- Toppings: fresh blueberries, sliced almonds, shredded coconut, granola, or additional honey

**Instructions:**

1. In a blender, combine the frozen blueberries, sliced banana, almond milk, rolled oats, almond butter, honey or maple syrup, and chia seeds.

2. Blend until smooth and creamy, adding more almond milk if needed to reach your desired consistency.

3. Pour the blueberry almond smoothie into a bowl.

4. Top with fresh blueberries, sliced almonds, shredded coconut, granola, or additional honey, as desired.

5. Serve the smoothie bowl immediately and enjoy!

## 3.9 Veggie Breakfast Burritos with Black Beans and Salsa

**Ingredients:**

- 4 large whole wheat tortillas
- 200 grams black beans, cooked and drained
- 1 bell pepper, diced (about 150 grams)
- 1 small onion, diced (about 100 grams)
- 100 grams cherry tomatoes, diced
- 100 grams baby spinach leaves
- 4 large eggs, scrambled
- 100 grams shredded cheddar cheese
- Salt and pepper to taste
- Olive oil or cooking spray, for sautéing
- Salsa, for serving

**Instructions:**

1. Heat a non-stick skillet over medium heat. Add a little olive oil or cooking spray.

2. Sauté the diced bell pepper and onion until softened, about 3-4 minutes.

3. Add the cherry tomatoes and baby spinach leaves to the skillet. Cook until the spinach wilts and the tomatoes soften slightly, about 1-2 minutes.

4. Push the vegetables to one side of the skillet and add the scrambled eggs to the other side. Cook, stirring occasionally, until the eggs are set.

5. Warm the whole wheat tortillas in a separate skillet or in the microwave.

6. To assemble the breakfast burritos, divide the scrambled eggs and sautéed vegetables evenly among the tortillas.

7. Top each with cooked black beans and shredded cheddar cheese.

8. Season with salt and pepper to taste.

9. Roll up the tortillas, tucking in the sides as you go, to form burritos.

10. Serve the veggie breakfast burritos with salsa on the side for dipping. Enjoy!

## 3.10 Whole Grain Pancakes with Fresh Berries and Maple Syrup

**Ingredients:**

- 150 grams whole wheat flour
- 50 grams rolled oats
- 2 tablespoons ground flaxseed
- 2 teaspoons baking powder
- 1/4 teaspoon salt
- 1 tablespoon honey or maple syrup
- 1 egg
- 240 milliliters almond milk or any milk of your choice
- 1 tablespoon melted coconut oil or butter, plus more for cooking
- Fresh berries (such as strawberries, blueberries, or raspberries), for serving
- Maple syrup, for serving

**Instructions:**

1. In a large mixing bowl, whisk together the whole wheat flour, rolled oats, ground flaxseed, baking powder, and salt.

2. In a separate bowl, beat the egg with the honey or maple syrup, almond milk, and melted coconut oil or butter.

3. Pour the wet ingredients into the dry ingredients and stir until just combined. Be careful not to overmix; a few lumps are okay.

4. Heat a non-stick skillet or griddle over medium heat and lightly grease with coconut oil or butter.

5. Pour a small amount of pancake batter onto the skillet for each pancake, using about 1/4 cup of batter per pancake.

6. Cook for 2-3 minutes, or until bubbles form on the surface of the pancakes and the edges start to look set.

7. Flip the pancakes and cook for another 1-2 minutes, or until golden brown and cooked through.

8. Repeat with the remaining batter, greasing the skillet as needed.

9. Serve the whole grain pancakes warm, topped with fresh berries and a drizzle of maple syrup. Enjoy!

## 3.11 Greek Yogurt Parfait with Granola and Mixed Berries

**Ingredients:**

- 200 grams Greek yogurt
- 50 grams granola
- 100 grams mixed berries (such as strawberries, blueberries, and raspberries)
- 1 tablespoon honey or maple syrup (optional)

**Instructions:**

1. In a glass or bowl, layer the Greek yogurt, granola, and mixed berries.

2. If desired, drizzle honey or maple syrup over the top for added sweetness.

3. Repeat the layers until the glass or bowl is filled, ending with a layer of mixed berries on top.

4. Serve the Greek yogurt parfait immediately as a delicious and nutritious breakfast or snack. Enjoy!

## 3.12   Veggie and Cheese Breakfast Quesadillas

**Ingredients:**

- 4 large whole wheat tortillas
- 100 grams shredded cheddar cheese
- 1 bell pepper, diced (about 150 grams)
- 1 small onion, diced (about 100 grams)
- 100 grams mushrooms, sliced
- 1 cup baby spinach leaves
- 4 large eggs, scrambled
- Salt and pepper to taste
- Olive oil or cooking spray, for sautéing

**Instructions:**

1. Heat a non-stick skillet over medium heat. Add a little olive oil or cooking spray.

2. Sauté the diced bell pepper, onion, and mushrooms until softened, about 3-4 minutes. Add the baby spinach leaves to the skillet and cook until wilted, about 1-2 minutes.

3. Push the vegetables to one side of the skillet and add the scrambled eggs to the other side. Cook, stirring occasionally, until the eggs are set.

4. Warm the whole wheat tortillas in a separate skillet or in the microwave.

5. To assemble the breakfast quesadillas, divide the shredded cheddar cheese evenly among the tortillas.

6. Top each tortilla with the cooked vegetable and egg mixture.Season with salt and pepper to taste.

7. Fold the tortillas in half to form quesadillas.

8. Heat a clean skillet over medium heat. Place the quesadillas in the skillet and cook for 2-3 minutes on each side, or until golden brown and the cheese is melted.

9. Remove the quesadillas from the skillet and let them cool slightly before slicing into wedges.

10. Serve the veggie and cheese breakfast quesadillas hot, with salsa or sour cream on the side if desired. Enjoy!

## 3.13 Smoked Salmon Bagel with Cream Cheese, Red Onion, and Capers

**Ingredients:**

- 1 whole grain bagel
- 50 grams smoked salmon
- 2 tablespoons cream cheese
- 1/4 red onion, thinly sliced
- 1 tablespoon capers
- Fresh dill, for garnish (optional)

**Instructions:**

1. Slice the whole grain bagel in half and toast it to your desired level of crispiness.

2. Spread cream cheese evenly on each half of the toasted bagel.

3. Top one half of the bagel with smoked salmon slices.

4. Arrange the thinly sliced red onion and capers over the smoked salmon.

5. Garnish with fresh dill, if desired.

6. Place the other half of the bagel on top to form a sandwich.

7. Serve the smoked salmon bagel immediately for a delicious and satisfying breakfast. Enjoy!

## 3.14  Breakfast Tacos with Scrambled Eggs, Avocado, and Salsa

**Ingredients:**

- 4 small corn tortillas
- 4 large eggs
- 1 ripe avocado, sliced
- 1/2 cup salsa
- Salt and pepper to taste
- Olive oil or cooking spray, for cooking

**Instructions:**

1. Warm the corn tortillas in a skillet over medium heat until they are soft and pliable. Set aside and keep warm.

2. In a bowl, whisk the eggs until well beaten. Season with salt and pepper to taste.

3. Heat a non-stick skillet over medium heat. Add a little olive oil or cooking spray.

4. Pour the beaten eggs into the skillet and cook, stirring occasionally, until they are scrambled and cooked through.

5. Divide the scrambled eggs evenly among the warm corn tortillas.

6. Top each taco with sliced avocado and salsa.

7. Serve the breakfast tacos immediately for a delicious and satisfying morning meal. Enjoy!

## 3.15 Breakfast Quinoa Bowl with Mixed Berries and Almonds

**Ingredients:**

- 100 grams quinoa
- 200 milliliters almond milk or any milk of your choice
- 1 tablespoon honey or maple syrup
- 100 grams mixed berries (such as strawberries, blueberries, and raspberries)
- 30 grams sliced almonds
- Optional toppings: Greek yogurt, chia seeds, or cinnamon

**Instructions:**

1. Rinse the quinoa under cold water using a fine mesh sieve.

2. In a saucepan, combine the rinsed quinoa and almond milk. Bring to a boil over medium heat.

3. Reduce the heat to low, cover, and simmer for 15-20 minutes, or until the quinoa is cooked and the liquid is absorbed.

4. Fluff the quinoa with a fork and stir in the honey or maple syrup.

5. Divide the cooked quinoa into serving bowls.

6. Top each bowl with mixed berries and sliced almonds.

7. If desired, add additional toppings such as Greek yogurt, chia seeds, or a sprinkle of cinnamon.

8. Serve the breakfast quinoa bowls warm and enjoy a nutritious start to your day!

# Chapter 4: Satisfying Lunches and Dinners to Support Blood Sugar Balance

From vibrant salads bursting with a rainbow of vegetables to hearty mains brimming with satisfying flavors, each dish in this chapter stands as a testament to the perfect harmony between culinary creativity and blood sugar balance.

At the heart of this chapter is a dedication to holistic well-being, with every recipe designed to prioritize stable blood sugar levels while delivering exceptional taste and satisfaction. Whether you're craving a comforting bowl of soup to warm you up or a refreshing stir-fry to energize your day, you'll discover a diverse range of options that are both delicious and supportive of your health goals. Each recipe is crafted to demonstrate that maintaining blood sugar balance can be both enjoyable and rewarding.

As you explore this collection, prepare to be inspired by the vibrant flavors, enticing aromas, and nourishing ingredients that fill these pages. Whether you're cooking for yourself, your family, or friends, these recipes offer a gateway to delicious, blood sugar-friendly meals that also support your overall well-being. With a focus on simplicity, flavor, and health.

## 4.1   Grilled Salmon with Lemon-Dill Sauce

**Ingredients:**

- 4 salmon fillets (about 150 grams each)
- 2 tablespoons olive oil
- 2 tablespoons lemon juice
- 2 cloves garlic, minced
- 1 tablespoon chopped fresh dill
- Salt and pepper to taste

**Instructions:**

1. Preheat the grill to medium-high heat.

2. In a small bowl, whisk together the olive oil, lemon juice, minced garlic, chopped fresh dill, salt, and pepper.

3. Place the salmon fillets on a plate and brush both sides with the lemon-dill marinade.

4. Place the salmon fillets on the preheated grill and cook for 4-5 minutes per side, or until the salmon is cooked through and flakes easily with a fork.

5. Remove the salmon from the grill and transfer to a serving platter.

6. Serve the grilled salmon hot, garnished with additional fresh dill if desired. Enjoy!

## 4.2 Quinoa and Black Bean Stuffed Bell Peppers

**Ingredients:**

- 4 large bell peppers (any color)
- 185 grams quinoa
- 400 grams black beans, drained and rinsed
- 150 grams corn kernels (fresh, frozen, or canned)
- 1 small onion, diced
- 2 cloves garlic, minced
- 1 teaspoon ground cumin
- 1 teaspoon chili powder
- Salt and pepper to taste
- 115 grams shredded cheddar cheese (optional)
- Fresh cilantro, chopped, for garnish

**Instructions:**

1. Preheat the oven to 375°F (190°C). Grease a baking dish with non-stick cooking spray.

2. Cut the tops off the bell peppers and remove the seeds and membranes. Place the bell peppers upright in the prepared baking dish.

3. In a saucepan, combine the quinoa and 470 milliliters of water. Bring to a boil, then reduce the heat to low, cover, and simmer for 15-20 minutes, or until the quinoa is cooked and the water is absorbed.

4. In a large skillet, heat some olive oil over medium heat. Add the diced onion and cook until softened, about 5 minutes. Add the minced garlic, ground cumin, and chili powder, and cook for another minute.

5. Stir in the cooked quinoa, black beans, corn kernels, salt, and pepper. Cook for 2-3 minutes to heat everything through.

6. Spoon the quinoa and black bean mixture into the hollowed-out bell peppers, filling them to the top. If using, sprinkle shredded cheddar cheese over the tops of the stuffed peppers.

7. Cover the baking dish with foil and bake in the preheated oven for 25-30 minutes, or until the peppers are tender.

8. Remove the foil and bake for an additional 5-10 minutes, or until the cheese is melted and bubbly.Remove the stuffed bell peppers from the oven and let them cool for a few minutes before serving.

9. Garnish with chopped fresh cilantro before serving. Enjoy!

## 4.3  Chicken and Vegetable Stir-Fry with Brown Rice

**Ingredients:**

- 250 grams boneless, skinless chicken breast, thinly sliced
- 200 grams brown rice
- 200 grams broccoli florets
- 150 grams carrots, thinly sliced
- 150 grams bell peppers, thinly sliced
- 100 grams snow peas
- 2 cloves garlic, minced
- 1 tablespoon ginger, minced
- 3 tablespoons soy sauce
- 1 tablespoon oyster sauce
- 1 tablespoon sesame oil
- 1 tablespoon olive oil
- Salt and pepper to taste
- Sesame seeds, for garnish (optional)
- Green onions, chopped, for garnish (optional)

**Instructions:**

1. Cook the brown rice according to package instructions. Once cooked, set aside and keep warm.

2. In a small bowl, mix together the soy sauce, oyster sauce, and sesame oil. Set aside.

3. Heat olive oil in a large skillet or wok over medium-high heat. Add the sliced chicken breast and cook until browned and cooked through, about 4-5 minutes. Remove from the skillet and set aside.

4. In the same skillet, add a little more olive oil if needed. Add the minced garlic and ginger, and cook for about 30 seconds, or until fragrant.

5. Add the broccoli, carrots, bell peppers, and snow peas to the skillet. Stir-fry for 3-4 minutes, or until the vegetables are crisp-tender.

6. Return the cooked chicken to the skillet. Pour the sauce over the chicken and vegetables, and toss everything together until well coated. Cook for another 2-3 minutes.

7. Season with salt and pepper to taste.

8. Serve the chicken and vegetable stir-fry over the cooked brown rice.

9. Garnish with sesame seeds and chopped green onions, if desired.

10. Enjoy your delicious and nutritious chicken and vegetable stir-fry!

## 4.4   Lentil Soup with Spinach and Turmeric

**Ingredients:**

- 200 grams dried lentils
- 1 onion, diced
- 2 cloves garlic, minced
- 1 carrot, diced
- 1 celery stalk, diced
- 100 grams fresh spinach leaves
- 1 teaspoon ground turmeric
- 1 teaspoon ground cumin
- 1/2 teaspoon ground coriander
- 1/4 teaspoon cayenne pepper (optional)
- 1 bay leaf
- 1.5 liters vegetable or chicken broth
- Salt and pepper to taste
- 2 tablespoons olive oil
- Fresh parsley, chopped, for garnish (optional)

**Instructions:**

1. Rinse the lentils under cold water and set aside.

2. Heat olive oil in a large pot over medium heat. Add the diced onion, garlic, carrot, and celery. Cook, stirring occasionally, until the vegetables are softened, about 5-7 minutes.

3. Add the ground turmeric, cumin, coriander, and cayenne pepper (if using) to the pot. Stir to coat the vegetables in the spices and cook for another minute until fragrant.

4. Add the rinsed lentils, bay leaf, and vegetable or chicken broth to the pot. Bring the soup to a boil, then reduce the heat to low and let it simmer, partially covered, for about 25-30 minutes, or until the lentils are tender.

5. Stir in the fresh spinach leaves and cook for an additional 2-3 minutes, or until the spinach is wilted.

6. Season the soup with salt and pepper to taste.

7. Remove the bay leaf before serving.

8. Ladle the lentil soup into bowls and garnish with fresh chopped parsley, if desired.

9. Serve hot and enjoy this comforting and nutritious lentil soup!

## 4.5   Baked Cod with Mediterranean Salsa

**Ingredients:**

- 4 cod fillets (about 150 grams each)
- 30 milliliters olive oil
- 2 cloves garlic, minced
- 1 teaspoon dried oregano
- 1/2 teaspoon dried thyme
- Salt and pepper to taste
- 2 tomatoes, diced (about 250 grams)
- 1/2 cucumber, diced (about 100 grams)
- 1/4 red onion, finely chopped (about 50 grams)
- 60 grams Kalamata olives, pitted and chopped
- 30 milliliters fresh lemon juice
- 15 grams chopped fresh parsley
- 15 grams chopped fresh basil

**Instructions:**

1. Preheat the oven to 375°F (190°C). Grease a baking dish with olive oil or non-stick cooking spray.

2. Pat the cod fillets dry with paper towels and place them in the prepared baking dish.

3. In a small bowl, mix together 15 milliliters of olive oil, minced garlic, dried oregano, dried thyme, salt, and pepper. Brush the mixture over the cod fillets.

4. Bake the cod in the preheated oven for 15-20 minutes, or until the fish is opaque and flakes easily with a fork.

5. While the cod is baking, prepare the Mediterranean salsa. In a medium bowl, combine the diced tomatoes, diced cucumber, finely chopped red onion, chopped Kalamata olives, fresh lemon juice, remaining 15 milliliters of olive oil, chopped fresh parsley, and chopped fresh basil. Season with salt and pepper to taste.

6. Once the cod is cooked, remove it from the oven and let it rest for a few minutes.

7. Serve the baked cod fillets topped with the Mediterranean salsa.

8. Enjoy this flavorful and nutritious dish!

## 4.6   Turkey and Vegetable Meatloaf

**Ingredients:**

- 500 grams ground turkey
- 1 onion, finely chopped
- 2 cloves garlic, minced
- 1 carrot, grated
- 1 zucchini, grated
- 1/2 red bell pepper, finely chopped
- 1/2 green bell pepper, finely chopped
- 1/4 cup breadcrumbs
- 1/4 cup grated Parmesan cheese
- 1 egg
- 2 tablespoons tomato paste
- 1 tablespoon Worcestershire sauce
- 1 teaspoon dried thyme
- 1 teaspoon dried oregano
- Salt and pepper to taste

**Instructions:**

1. Preheat the oven to 375°F (190°C). Grease a loaf pan with olive oil or non-stick cooking spray.

2. In a large mixing bowl, combine the ground turkey, finely chopped onion, minced garlic, grated carrot, grated zucchini, finely chopped red bell pepper, finely chopped green bell pepper, breadcrumbs, grated Parmesan cheese, egg, tomato paste, Worcestershire sauce, dried thyme, dried oregano, salt, and pepper. Mix until all ingredients are well combined.

3. Transfer the turkey mixture into the prepared loaf pan, pressing it down evenly with a spatula.

4. Bake the meatloaf in the preheated oven for 45-50 minutes, or until cooked through and golden brown on top.

5. Remove the meatloaf from the oven and let it rest for 5-10 minutes before slicing.

6. Serve slices of the turkey and vegetable meatloaf with your favorite sides, such as mashed potatoes and steamed vegetables.

7. Enjoy this nutritious twist on a classic comfort food dish!

## 4.7  Veggie-loaded Pasta Primavera

**Ingredients:**

- 250 grams whole wheat pasta
- 2 tablespoons olive oil
- 2 cloves garlic, minced
- 1 onion, thinly sliced
- 1 carrot, julienned
- 1 zucchini, julienned
- 1 yellow bell pepper, thinly sliced
- 1 red bell pepper, thinly sliced
- 100 grams cherry tomatoes, halved
- 1/2 cup vegetable broth
- 1/4 cup grated Parmesan cheese
- 2 tablespoons chopped fresh basil
- Salt and pepper to taste

**Instructions:**

1. Cook the whole wheat pasta according to package instructions until al dente. Drain and set aside.

2. In a large skillet, heat the olive oil over medium heat. Add the minced garlic and thinly sliced onion, and sauté until softened and fragrant, about 2-3 minutes.

3. Add the julienned carrot, julienned zucchini, and thinly sliced bell peppers to the skillet. Sauté for 4-5 minutes, or until the vegetables are tender-crisp.

4. Stir in the halved cherry tomatoes and vegetable broth. Cook for another 2-3 minutes, allowing the tomatoes to soften slightly and the flavors to meld together.

5. Add the cooked whole wheat pasta to the skillet, tossing everything together until well combined.

6. Season the pasta primavera with salt and pepper to taste. Sprinkle grated Parmesan cheese and chopped fresh basil over the top.

7. Serve the veggie-loaded pasta primavera hot, garnished with additional grated Parmesan cheese and fresh basil if desired.

8. Enjoy this vibrant and nutritious pasta dish bursting with the flavors of spring vegetables!

## 4.8 Beef and Broccoli Stir-Fry with Garlic Sauce

**Ingredients:**

- 300 grams beef sirloin, thinly sliced
- 2 tablespoons soy sauce
- 1 tablespoon oyster sauce
- 1 tablespoon cornstarch
- 2 tablespoons olive oil
- 3 cloves garlic, minced
- 1 head broccoli, cut into florets
- 1 carrot, thinly sliced
- 1/2 onion, thinly sliced
- 1/4 cup beef broth
- 1 tablespoon honey or brown sugar
- Salt and pepper to taste
- Sesame seeds, for garnish (optional)
- Sliced green onions, for garnish (optional)

**Instructions:**

1. In a bowl, marinate the thinly sliced beef sirloin with soy sauce, oyster sauce, and cornstarch. Let it sit for 15-20 minutes.

2. Heat olive oil in a large skillet or wok over medium-high heat. Add minced garlic and stir-fry for about 30 seconds until fragrant.

3. Add the marinated beef slices to the skillet and stir-fry until they are browned and cooked through, about 2-3 minutes. Remove the beef from the skillet and set aside.

4. In the same skillet, add the broccoli florets, sliced carrot, and thinly sliced onion. Stir-fry for about 4-5 minutes until the vegetables are tender-crisp.

5. Return the cooked beef to the skillet. Add beef broth and honey or brown sugar, stirring to combine. Cook for another 2-3 minutes until the sauce thickens slightly.

6. Season with salt and pepper to taste.

7. Serve the beef and broccoli stir-fry hot, garnished with sesame seeds and sliced green onions if desired.

8. Enjoy this flavorful and nutritious stir-fry with garlic sauce!

## 4.9  Moroccan Chickpea Stew with Couscous

**Ingredients:**

- 1 tablespoon olive oil
- 1 onion, finely chopped
- 2 cloves garlic, minced
- 1 carrot, diced
- 1 bell pepper, diced
- 1 zucchini, diced
- 1 can (400 grams) chickpeas, drained and rinsed
- 1 can (400 grams) diced tomatoes
- 2 cups vegetable broth
- 1 teaspoon ground cumin
- 1 teaspoon ground coriander
- 1/2 teaspoon ground cinnamon
- 1/4 teaspoon cayenne pepper (optional)
- Salt and pepper to taste
- 1 cup couscous
- Fresh cilantro, chopped, for garnish
- Lemon wedges, for serving

**Instructions:**

1. Heat olive oil in a large pot over medium heat. Add the finely chopped onion and minced garlic, and sauté until softened and fragrant, about 2-3 minutes.

2. Add the diced carrot, bell pepper, and zucchini to the pot. Cook, stirring occasionally, for about 5 minutes until the vegetables start to soften.

3. Stir in the drained and rinsed chickpeas, diced tomatoes, vegetable broth, ground cumin, ground coriander, ground cinnamon, and cayenne pepper (if using). Season with salt and pepper to taste.

4. Bring the stew to a simmer, then reduce the heat to low and let it simmer for 15-20 minutes, allowing the flavors to meld together.

5. While the stew is simmering, prepare the couscous according to package instructions.

6. Fluff the cooked couscous with a fork and divide it among serving bowls. Ladle the Moroccan chickpea stew over the couscous.

7. Garnish with chopped fresh cilantro and serve with lemon wedges on the side.

8. Enjoy this hearty and aromatic Moroccan chickpea stew with couscous!

# 4.10 Grilled Vegetable Platter with Balsamic Glaze

**Ingredients:**

- 1 zucchini, sliced lengthwise
- 1 yellow squash, sliced lengthwise
- 1 eggplant, sliced into rounds
- 1 red bell pepper, seeded and quartered
- 1 yellow bell pepper, seeded and quartered
- 1 red onion, sliced into rounds
- 2 tablespoons olive oil
- Salt and pepper to taste
- Balsamic glaze, for drizzling
- Fresh basil leaves, for garnish

**Instructions:**

1. Preheat the grill to medium-high heat.

2. Brush the sliced zucchini, yellow squash, eggplant, red bell pepper, yellow bell pepper, and red onion rounds with olive oil. Season with salt and pepper to taste.

3. Place the vegetables on the preheated grill and cook for 3-4 minutes per side, or until they are tender and have grill marks.

4. Transfer the grilled vegetables to a serving platter.

5. Drizzle the grilled vegetable platter with balsamic glaze.

6. Garnish with fresh basil leaves.

7. Serve the grilled vegetable platter as a delicious and colorful side dish or appetizer.

8. Enjoy this flavorful and nutritious dish!

# 4.11   Shrimp and Avocado Salad with Lime Dressing

**Ingredients:**

- 200 grams shrimp, peeled and deveined
- 1 avocado, diced
- 1 cup cherry tomatoes, halved
- 1/4 cup red onion, thinly sliced
- 1/4 cup cucumber, diced
- 2 tablespoons fresh cilantro, chopped
- 1 lime, juiced
- 2 tablespoons olive oil
- Salt and pepper to taste

**Instructions:**

1. In a medium bowl, combine the peeled and deveined shrimp, diced avocado, halved cherry tomatoes, thinly sliced red onion, diced cucumber, and chopped fresh cilantro.

2. In a small bowl, whisk together the lime juice and olive oil to make the dressing. Season with salt and pepper to taste.

3. Pour the lime dressing over the shrimp and avocado mixture. Toss gently to coat everything evenly.

4. Serve the shrimp and avocado salad immediately, garnished with additional fresh cilantro if desired.

5. Enjoy this refreshing and flavorful salad as a light and healthy meal!

## 4.12 Stuffed Portobello Mushrooms with Quinoa and Feta

**Ingredients:**

- 4 large Portobello mushrooms
- 200 grams cooked quinoa
- 100 grams crumbled feta cheese
- 15 grams chopped fresh parsley
- 2 cloves garlic, minced
- 30 milliliters olive oil
- Salt and pepper to taste

**Instructions:**

1. Preheat the oven to 375°F (190°C). Line a baking sheet with parchment paper.

2. Remove the stems from the Portobello mushrooms and gently scrape out the gills with a spoon. Place the mushrooms on the prepared baking sheet.

3. In a mixing bowl, combine the cooked quinoa, crumbled feta cheese, chopped fresh parsley, minced garlic, olive oil, salt, and pepper. Mix well to combine.

4. Divide the quinoa mixture evenly among the Portobello mushrooms, pressing it down gently into the caps.

5. Bake the stuffed Portobello mushrooms in the preheated oven for 20-25 minutes, or until the mushrooms are tender and the filling is heated through.

6. Serve the stuffed Portobello mushrooms hot, garnished with additional chopped parsley if desired.

7. Enjoy this flavorful and satisfying dish as a nutritious meal or appetizer!

## 4.13  Spaghetti Squash with Turkey Bolognese

**Ingredients:**

- 1 medium spaghetti squash
- 300 grams ground turkey
- 1 onion, diced
- 2 cloves garlic, minced
- 1 carrot, diced
- 1 celery stalk, diced
- 1 can (400 grams) crushed tomatoes
- 1 teaspoon dried oregano
- 1 teaspoon dried basil
- Salt and pepper to taste
- Grated Parmesan cheese, for serving
- Fresh basil leaves, for garnish

**Instructions:**

1. Preheat the oven to 375°F (190°C). Cut the spaghetti squash in half lengthwise and scoop out the seeds with a spoon.

2. Place the squash halves, cut side down, on a baking sheet lined with parchment paper. Bake in the preheated oven for 35-45 minutes, or until the squash is tender and the flesh can be easily pierced with a fork. Remove from the oven and let cool slightly.

3. While the squash is baking, prepare the turkey bolognese sauce. In a large skillet, heat some olive oil over medium heat. Add the diced onion, minced garlic, diced carrot, and diced celery. Cook until the vegetables are softened, about 5-7 minutes.

4. Add the ground turkey to the skillet and cook until browned, breaking it up with a spoon as it cooks.

5. Stir in the crushed tomatoes, dried oregano, dried basil, salt, and pepper. Simmer the sauce for 15-20 minutes, stirring occasionally, until the flavors are well combined.

6. Use a fork to scrape the spaghetti squash flesh into strands. Divide the squash strands among serving plates.

7. Top the spaghetti squash with the turkey bolognese sauce. Serve hot, garnished with grated Parmesan cheese and fresh basil leaves.

8. Enjoy this wholesome and delicious spaghetti squash with turkey bolognese as a nutritious meal!

## 4.14 Baked Chicken Parmesan with Whole Wheat Pasta

**Ingredients:**

- 2 boneless, skinless chicken breasts (about 300 grams each)
- 1/2 cup whole wheat breadcrumbs
- 1/4 cup grated Parmesan cheese
- 1 teaspoon dried oregano
- 1 teaspoon dried basil
- 1/2 teaspoon garlic powder
- Salt and pepper to taste
- 1 egg, beaten
- 1 cup marinara sauce
- 1/2 cup shredded mozzarella cheese
- 200 grams whole wheat pasta
- Fresh basil leaves, for garnish

**Instructions:**

1. Preheat the oven to 400°F (200°C). Grease a baking dish with olive oil or non-stick cooking spray.

2. In a shallow dish, combine the whole wheat breadcrumbs, grated Parmesan cheese, dried oregano, dried basil, garlic powder, salt, and pepper.

3. Dip each chicken breast in the beaten egg, then coat it with the breadcrumb mixture, pressing gently to adhere.

4. Place the breaded chicken breasts in the prepared baking dish. Bake in the preheated oven for 20-25 minutes, or until the chicken is cooked through and the coating is golden brown.

5. Spoon marinara sauce over the baked chicken breasts, then sprinkle shredded mozzarella cheese on top.

6. Return the baking dish to the oven and bake for an additional 5-10 minutes, or until the cheese is melted and bubbly.

7. While the chicken is baking, cook the whole wheat pasta according to package instructions until al dente. Drain and set aside.

8. Serve the baked chicken Parmesan hot, alongside whole wheat pasta. Garnish with fresh basil leaves.

9. Enjoy this healthier twist on a classic Italian favorite!

## 4.15   Roasted Vegetable and Chickpea Buddha Bowl

**Ingredients:**

- 1 cup cooked quinoa
- 1 cup chickpeas, drained and rinsed
- 1 cup broccoli florets
- 1 cup cauliflower florets
- 1 red bell pepper, sliced
- 1 yellow bell pepper, sliced
- 1 carrot, sliced into matchsticks
- 2 tablespoons olive oil
- 1 teaspoon ground cumin
- 1 teaspoon smoked paprika
- Salt and pepper to taste
- Tahini dressing, for serving
- Fresh parsley, chopped, for garnish

**Instructions:**

1. Preheat the oven to 400°F (200°C). Line a baking sheet with parchment paper.

2. In a large mixing bowl, toss together the cooked quinoa, chickpeas, broccoli florets, cauliflower florets, sliced red bell pepper, sliced yellow bell pepper, and sliced carrot.

3. Drizzle olive oil over the vegetables and chickpeas, then sprinkle with ground cumin, smoked paprika, salt, and pepper. Toss to coat everything evenly.

4. Spread the seasoned vegetables and chickpeas in a single layer on the prepared baking sheet.

5. Roast in the preheated oven for 20-25 minutes, or until the vegetables are tender and lightly browned.

6. Divide the roasted vegetable and chickpea mixture among serving bowls. Drizzle with tahini dressing.

7. Garnish with chopped fresh parsley before serving.

8. Enjoy this nourishing and flavorful roasted vegetable and chickpea Buddha bowl!

# 4.16   Tofu and Vegetable Curry with Coconut Milk

**Ingredients:**

- 200 grams firm tofu, cubed
- 1 tablespoon olive oil
- 1 onion, chopped
- 2 cloves garlic, minced
- 1 tablespoon curry powder
- 1 teaspoon ground turmeric
- 1 teaspoon ground cumin
- 1/2 teaspoon ground coriander
- 1/4 teaspoon cayenne pepper (optional)
- 1 can (400 ml) coconut milk
- 2 cups mixed vegetables (such as bell peppers, broccoli, carrots, and peas)
- Salt and pepper to taste
- Cooked rice, for serving
- Fresh cilantro, chopped, for garnish

**Instructions:**

1. Heat olive oil in a large skillet or saucepan over medium heat. Add the chopped onion and minced garlic, and sauté until softened and fragrant, about 2-3 minutes.

2. Add the cubed tofu to the skillet and cook until lightly browned on all sides, about 5-7 minutes.

3. Stir in the curry powder, ground turmeric, ground cumin, ground coriander, and cayenne pepper (if using). Cook for another minute until the spices are fragrant.

4. Pour in the coconut milk and bring the mixture to a simmer.

5. Add the mixed vegetables to the skillet and stir to combine. Simmer for 10-15 minutes, or until the vegetables are tender.

6. Season the tofu and vegetable curry with salt and pepper to taste.

7. Serve the tofu and vegetable curry hot, over cooked rice.

8. Garnish with chopped fresh cilantro before serving.

9. Enjoy this comforting and aromatic tofu and vegetable curry with coconut milk!

## 4.17   Greek-inspired Chicken Souvlaki with Tzatziki Sauce

**Ingredients:**

- 2 boneless, skinless chicken breasts (about 300 grams each), cut into cubes
- 2 tablespoons olive oil
- 1 lemon, juiced
- 2 cloves garlic, minced
- 1 teaspoon dried oregano
- Salt and pepper to taste
- Tzatziki sauce, for serving
- Pita bread or cooked rice, for serving
- Sliced cucumber, tomato, and red onion, for garnish

**Instructions:**

1. In a bowl, combine the cubed chicken breasts, olive oil, lemon juice, minced garlic, dried oregano, salt, and pepper. Mix well to coat the chicken evenly. Cover and refrigerate for at least 30 minutes to marinate.

2. Preheat the grill or grill pan over medium-high heat. Thread the marinated chicken cubes onto skewers.

3. Grill the chicken skewers for 6-8 minutes per side, or until they are cooked through and have nice grill marks.

4. Serve the Greek-inspired chicken souvlaki hot, with tzatziki sauce on the side for dipping. Accompany with pita bread or cooked rice, and garnish with sliced cucumber, tomato, and red onion.

5. Enjoy this flavorful and satisfying Mediterranean dish!

## 4.18   Ratatouille with Herbed Couscous

**Ingredients:**

- 1 eggplant, diced
- 1 zucchini, diced
- 1 yellow squash, diced
- 1 red bell pepper, diced
- 1 yellow bell pepper, diced
- 1 onion, diced
- 2 cloves garlic, minced
- 2 cups diced tomatoes (fresh or canned)
- 2 tablespoons tomato paste
- 1 teaspoon dried thyme
- 1 teaspoon dried basil
- Salt and pepper to taste
- 1 cup couscous
- 1 1/4 cups vegetable broth
- Fresh parsley, chopped, for garnish

**Instructions:**

1. In a large skillet or saucepan, heat some olive oil over medium heat. Add the diced eggplant, zucchini, yellow squash, red bell pepper, yellow bell pepper, onion, and minced garlic. Cook until the vegetables are softened, about 8-10 minutes.

2. Stir in the diced tomatoes, tomato paste, dried thyme, dried basil, salt, and pepper. Simmer for another 10-15 minutes, until the flavors are well combined and the vegetables are tender.

3. While the ratatouille is simmering, prepare the herbed couscous. In a separate saucepan, bring the vegetable broth to a boil. Stir in the couscous, cover, and remove from heat. Let it sit for 5 minutes, then fluff the couscous with a fork.

4. Serve the ratatouille hot, over herbed couscous. Garnish with chopped fresh parsley.

5. Enjoy this comforting and colorful dish inspired by the flavors of the Mediterranean!

## 4.19 Beef and Vegetable Kabobs with Chimichurri Sauce

**Ingredients:**

- 300 grams beef sirloin, cut into cubes
- 1 red bell pepper, cut into chunks
- 1 green bell pepper, cut into chunks
- 1 red onion, cut into chunks
- 1 zucchini, sliced
- 1 yellow squash, sliced
- 2 tablespoons olive oil
- 2 cloves garlic, minced
- 1 teaspoon dried oregano
- Salt and pepper to taste
- Chimichurri sauce, for serving

**Instructions:**

1. In a bowl, combine the beef sirloin cubes, olive oil, minced garlic, dried oregano, salt, and pepper. Mix well to coat the beef evenly. Cover and refrigerate for at least 30 minutes to marinate.

2. Preheat the grill or grill pan over medium-high heat. Thread the marinated beef cubes and vegetable chunks onto skewers.

3. Grill the beef and vegetable kabobs for 8-10 minutes, turning occasionally, until the beef is cooked to your desired doneness and the vegetables are tender.

4. Serve the beef and vegetable kabobs hot, with chimichurri sauce on the side for dipping.

5. Enjoy these flavorful and colorful kabobs as a delicious and satisfying meal!

## 4.20   Sweet Potato and Black Bean Enchiladas

### Ingredients:

- 2 large sweet potatoes, peeled and diced
- 1 can (400 grams) black beans, drained and rinsed
- 1 red bell pepper, diced
- 1 onion, diced
- 2 cloves garlic, minced
- 1 teaspoon ground cumin
- 1 teaspoon chili powder
- Salt and pepper to taste
- 8 whole wheat tortillas
- 1 cup enchilada sauce
- 1 cup shredded cheese (such as Cheddar or Mexican blend)
- Fresh cilantro, chopped, for garnish
- Sour cream or Greek yogurt, for serving

### Instructions:

1. Preheat the oven to 375°F (190°C). Grease a 9x13-inch baking dish with olive oil or non-stick cooking spray.

2. In a large skillet, heat some olive oil over medium heat. Add the diced sweet potatoes and cook until softened, about 8-10 minutes.

3. Add the diced onion, minced garlic, and diced red bell pepper to the skillet. Cook until the vegetables are tender, about 5-7 minutes.

4. Stir in the drained black beans, ground cumin, chili powder, salt, and pepper. Cook for another 2-3 minutes, until the mixture is heated through and the flavors are well combined.

5. Place a spoonful of the sweet potato and black bean mixture onto each whole wheat tortilla. Roll up the tortillas and place them seam side down in the prepared baking dish.

6. Pour the enchilada sauce evenly over the rolled tortillas. Sprinkle shredded cheese on top.

7. Bake in the preheated oven for 20-25 minutes, or until the enchiladas are heated through and the cheese is melted and bubbly.

8. Serve the sweet potato and black bean enchiladas hot, garnished with chopped fresh cilantro. Serve with sour cream or Greek yogurt on the side if desired.

9. Enjoy these flavorful and satisfying enchiladas as a wholesome meal!

# Chapter 5: Smart Snacks and Desserts: Indulge Without Compromising Your Blood Sugar

In the realm of culinary pleasures, snacks and desserts often bring moments of joy and satisfaction to our busy lives. For those mindful of blood sugar levels, enjoying these treats can sometimes feel like a challenge. But it doesn't have to be this way. Welcome to a chapter that transforms the concept of snacks and desserts from occasional indulgences into essential components of a glucose-friendly diet.

Here, we embark on a journey that celebrates the art of creating smart snacks and satisfying desserts while keeping blood sugar balance as our priority. Say goodbye to feelings of restriction or guilt, and embrace a world of flavors, textures, and aromas that delight your taste buds and support your well-being from within.

Indulging in snacks and desserts can indeed be part of a balanced approach to managing blood sugar. In this chapter, we'll explore a range of delicious and nutritious options designed to support glucose regulation without compromising on taste.

From wholesome snacks to delightful desserts, these recipes feature ingredients that help stabilize blood sugar levels and promote overall health. Whether you're looking for a midday boost or a sweet treat to end your day, you'll find plenty of options that satisfy your cravings while supporting your glucose goals. Let's dive into a world where indulgence meets balance, and discover how to enjoy flavorful treats that align with your commitment to blood sugar management.

So, whether you're seeking a savory snack to tide you over or a sweet finish to your meal, rest assured that the recipes within these pages offer a satisfying way to indulge without compromising your health. Join us as we explore a culinary adventure where snacks and desserts are not just about temptation but about nourishing your body and achieving optimal blood sugar balance. Let's embark on this flavorful journey together, celebrating each bite as a step towards wellness, balance, and the joy of healthy living.

## 5.1   Dark Chocolate Avocado Mousse

**Ingredients:**

- 2 ripe avocados
- 50 grams dark chocolate, melted
- 30 grams cocoa powder
- 60 milliliters maple syrup or honey
- 1 teaspoon vanilla extract
- Pinch of salt

**Instructions:**

1. Scoop the flesh of the ripe avocados into a blender or food processor.

2. Add the melted dark chocolate, cocoa powder, maple syrup or honey, vanilla extract, and a pinch of salt to the blender.

3. Blend until smooth and creamy, scraping down the sides of the blender or food processor as needed.

4. Transfer the mousse to serving glasses or bowls.

5. Chill in the refrigerator for at least 30 minutes before serving.

6. Garnish with fresh berries, shaved chocolate, or a sprinkle of cocoa powder if desired.

7. Enjoy this decadent and creamy dark chocolate avocado mousse as a guilt-free dessert!

## 5.2   Baked Sweet Potato Chips with Sea Salt

**Ingredients:**

- 2 medium sweet potatoes, peeled and thinly sliced
- 30 grams olive oil
- Sea salt, to taste

**Instructions:**

1. Preheat the oven to 375°F (190°C). Line a baking sheet with parchment paper.

2. In a large bowl, toss the thinly sliced sweet potatoes with olive oil until evenly coated.

3. Spread the sweet potato slices in a single layer on the prepared baking sheet.

4. Bake in the preheated oven for 20-25 minutes, flipping halfway through, until the chips are crispy and golden brown.

5. Remove from the oven and sprinkle with sea salt to taste.

6. Allow the sweet potato chips to cool slightly before serving.

7. Enjoy these crunchy and flavorful baked sweet potato chips with sea salt as a wholesome snack or side dish!

## 5.3  Berry Almond Energy Bites

**Ingredients:**

- 100 grams almonds
- 100 grams dried mixed berries (such as cranberries, blueberries, and cherries)
- 50 grams rolled oats
- 30 grams almond butter
- 30 grams honey or maple syrup
- 1 teaspoon vanilla extract
- Pinch of salt

**Instructions:**

1. In a food processor, pulse the almonds until finely chopped.

2. Add the dried mixed berries and rolled oats to the food processor. Pulse until the mixture is well combined and the berries are finely chopped.

3. Add the almond butter, honey or maple syrup, vanilla extract, and a pinch of salt to the mixture in the food processor.

4. Pulse until the mixture comes together and forms a sticky dough.

5. Roll the dough into small balls, about 1 inch in diameter.

6. Place the energy bites on a baking sheet lined with parchment paper.

7. Chill in the refrigerator for at least 30 minutes before serving.

8. Enjoy these berry almond energy bites as a nutritious and energizing snack!

## 5.4 Greek Yogurt and Berry Popsicles

**Ingredients:**

- 200 grams Greek yogurt
- 100 grams mixed berries (such as strawberries, blueberries, and raspberries)
- 30 grams honey or maple syrup
- 1 teaspoon vanilla extract

**Instructions:**

1. In a blender or food processor, combine the Greek yogurt, mixed berries, honey or maple syrup, and vanilla extract.

2. Blend until smooth and well combined.

3. Pour the mixture into popsicle molds, leaving a little space at the top for expansion.

4. Insert popsicle sticks into the molds.

5. Freeze for at least 4 hours, or until the popsicles are completely frozen.

6. To unmold the popsicles, run the molds under warm water for a few seconds to loosen them.

7. Enjoy these refreshing Greek yogurt and berry popsicles as a cool and creamy treat!

## 5.5 Spiced Roasted Chickpeas

**Ingredients:**

- 400 grams canned chickpeas, drained and rinsed
- 15 grams olive oil
- 1 teaspoon ground cumin
- 1 teaspoon smoked paprika
- 1/2 teaspoon garlic powder
- 1/2 teaspoon onion powder
- Salt and pepper to taste

**Instructions:**

1. Preheat the oven to 400°F (200°C). Line a baking sheet with parchment paper.

2. Pat the drained and rinsed chickpeas dry with a clean kitchen towel or paper towels.

3. In a bowl, toss the chickpeas with olive oil, ground cumin, smoked paprika, garlic powder, onion powder, salt, and pepper until evenly coated.

4. Spread the seasoned chickpeas in a single layer on the prepared baking sheet.

5. Roast in the preheated oven for 20-25 minutes, shaking the pan halfway through, until the chickpeas are crispy and golden brown.

6. Remove from the oven and let cool slightly before serving.

7. Enjoy these spiced roasted chickpeas as a crunchy and flavorful snack!

## 5.6  Apple Slices with Almond Butter and Cinnamon

**Ingredients:**

- 2 medium apples, sliced
- 30 grams almond butter
- 5 grams honey or maple syrup (optional)
- Ground cinnamon, for sprinkling

**Instructions:**

1. Arrange the apple slices on a plate or serving platter.

2. In a small bowl, microwave the almond butter for a few seconds until it becomes slightly softened.

3. Drizzle the almond butter over the apple slices.

4. If desired, drizzle honey or maple syrup over the almond butter.

5. Sprinkle ground cinnamon over the apple slices.

6. Serve immediately and enjoy these apple slices with almond butter and cinnamon as a wholesome and satisfying snack!

## 5.7 No-Bake Oatmeal Raisin Cookie Energy Balls

**Ingredients:**

- 100 grams rolled oats
- 50 grams almond flour
- 50 grams raisins
- 30 grams honey or maple syrup
- 30 grams almond butter
- 1 teaspoon vanilla extract
- 1/2 teaspoon ground cinnamon
- Pinch of salt

**Instructions:**

1. In a large bowl, combine the rolled oats, almond flour, raisins, honey or maple syrup, almond butter, vanilla extract, ground cinnamon, and a pinch of salt.

2. Mix until all the ingredients are well combined and the mixture holds together.

3. Roll the mixture into small balls, about 1 inch in diameter.

4. Place the energy balls on a baking sheet lined with parchment paper.

5. Chill in the refrigerator for at least 30 minutes to firm up.

6. Enjoy these no-bake oatmeal raisin cookie energy balls as a nutritious and energizing snack!

## 5.8   Mango Coconut Chia Pudding

**Ingredients:**

- 200 grams ripe mango, diced
- 200 milliliters coconut milk
- 30 grams chia seeds
- 5 grams honey or maple syrup
- 1/2 teaspoon vanilla extract

**Instructions:**

1. In a blender or food processor, puree the ripe mango until smooth.

2. In a bowl, combine the mango puree, coconut milk, chia seeds, honey or maple syrup, and vanilla extract. Mix well.

3. Cover the bowl and refrigerate for at least 4 hours or overnight, allowing the chia seeds to thicken and the flavors to meld.

4. Stir the chia pudding before serving to ensure an even consistency.

5. Divide the mango coconut chia pudding into serving cups or jars.

6. Enjoy this creamy and tropical dessert as a delightful and nutritious treat!

## 5.9   Veggie Sticks with Hummus

**Ingredients:**

- 200 grams mixed veggie sticks (such as carrots, celery, cucumber, and bell peppers)
- 100 grams hummus

**Instructions:**

1. Wash and prepare the mixed veggie sticks by cutting them into sticks or bite-sized pieces.

2. Place the veggie sticks on a serving platter or plate. Serve the veggie sticks with hummus for dipping.

3. Enjoy these crunchy and flavorful veggie sticks with hummus as a healthy and satisfying snack!

# 5.10   Frozen Banana Bites with Peanut Butter Drizzle

**Ingredients:**

- 2 ripe bananas
- 50 grams peanut butter
- 30 grams dark chocolate, melted (optional)
- 10 grams chopped nuts (such as almonds, peanuts, or walnuts) (optional)

**Instructions:**

1. Peel the ripe bananas and slice them into bite-sized rounds.

2. Place the banana slices on a baking sheet lined with parchment paper.

3. Using a small spoon or knife, drizzle peanut butter over each banana slice.

4. If desired, drizzle melted dark chocolate over the banana slices.

5. Sprinkle chopped nuts over the banana slices for added crunch and flavor.

6. Place the baking sheet in the freezer and freeze the banana bites for at least 2 hours, or until firm.

7. Once frozen, transfer the banana bites to a container or resealable bag for storage in the freezer.

8. Serve the frozen banana bites with peanut butter drizzle straight from the freezer as a delicious and refreshing snack or dessert!

# What's Next? Grab Your Free Bonuses!

## Step 1

Scan the QR-code or visit the following website:

https://www.lucyevans.shop/glucose-revolution-cookbook-welcome

## Step 2:

Leave your data and get access to the bonuses included with any purchase of this book

## Step 3:

Leave an honest review on Amazon, your support will make the difference!

## Step 4:

Want more of my books? Here a wide selection of lovely crafted books available on Amazon!